M000312928

001
Wild turnip

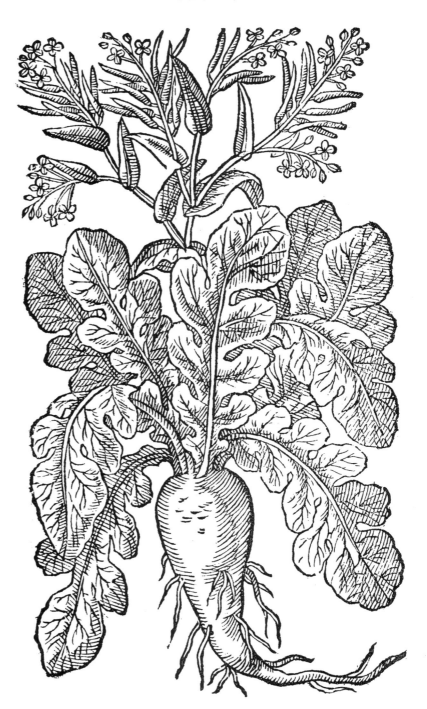

003
Navew-gentle

002
Lion's leaf
or lion's turnip

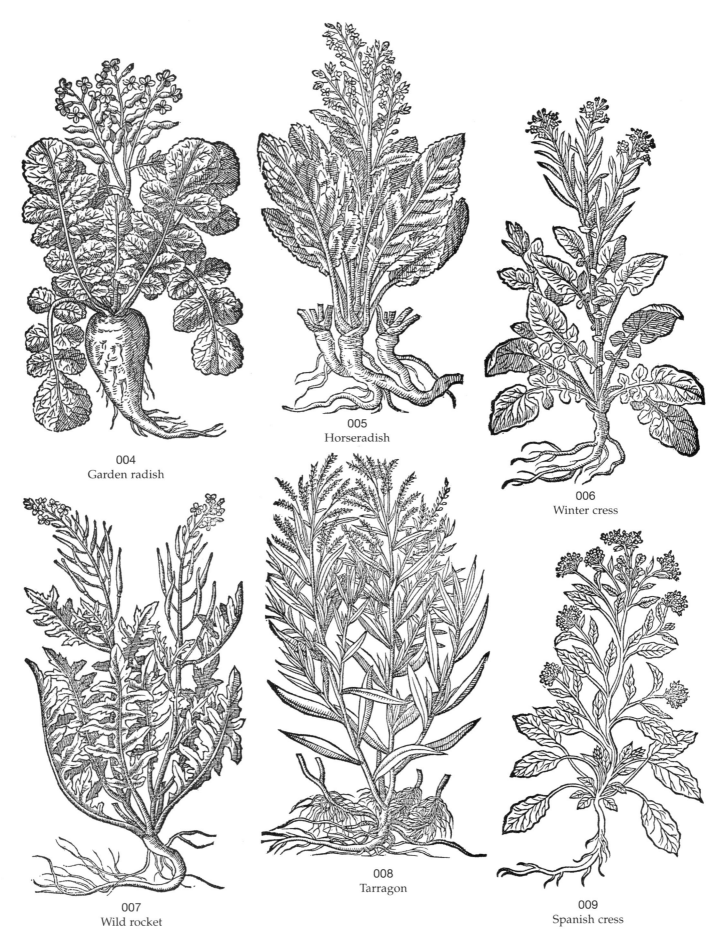

004
Garden radish

005
Horseradish

006
Winter cress

007
Wild rocket

008
Tarragon

009
Spanish cress

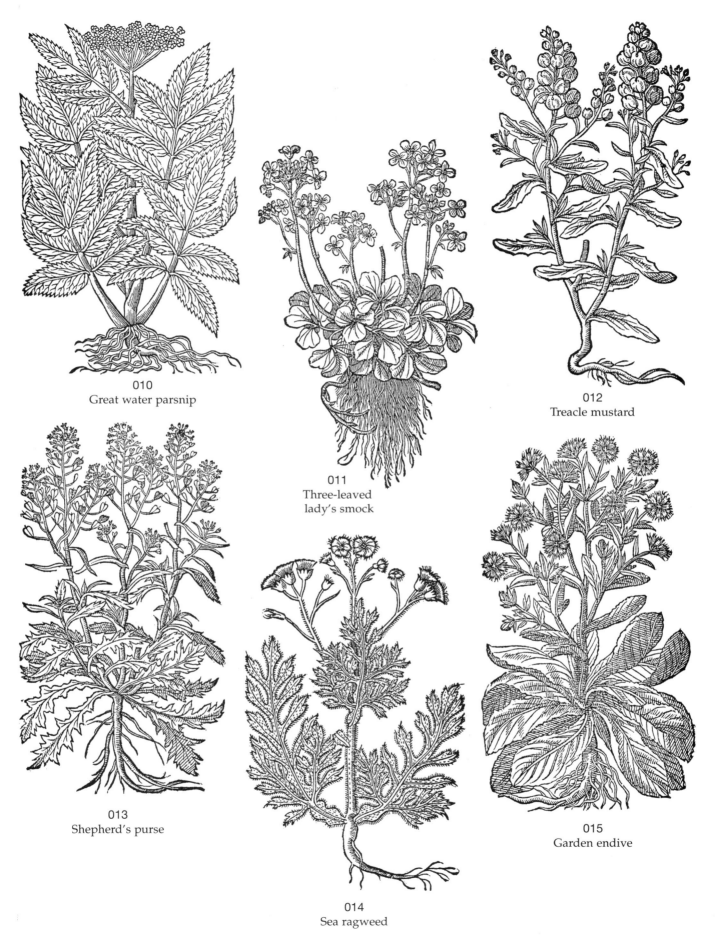

010
Great water parsnip

011
Three-leaved
lady's smock

012
Treacle mustard

013
Shepherd's purse

014
Sea ragweed

015
Garden endive

016
Wild chicory

017
Broad-leaved sow thistle

018
Knotty-rooted dandelion

019
Golden mouse-ear

4

020
Open cabbage cole

021
Lamb's lettuce

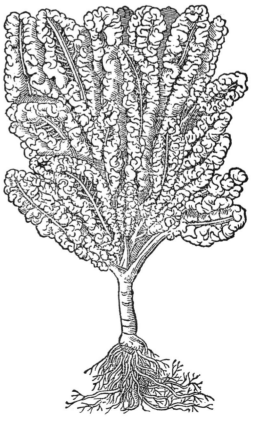

022
Swollen colewort

023
Red Roman beet

024
Branched flower-gentle

025
Great white blite

026
Sea orach

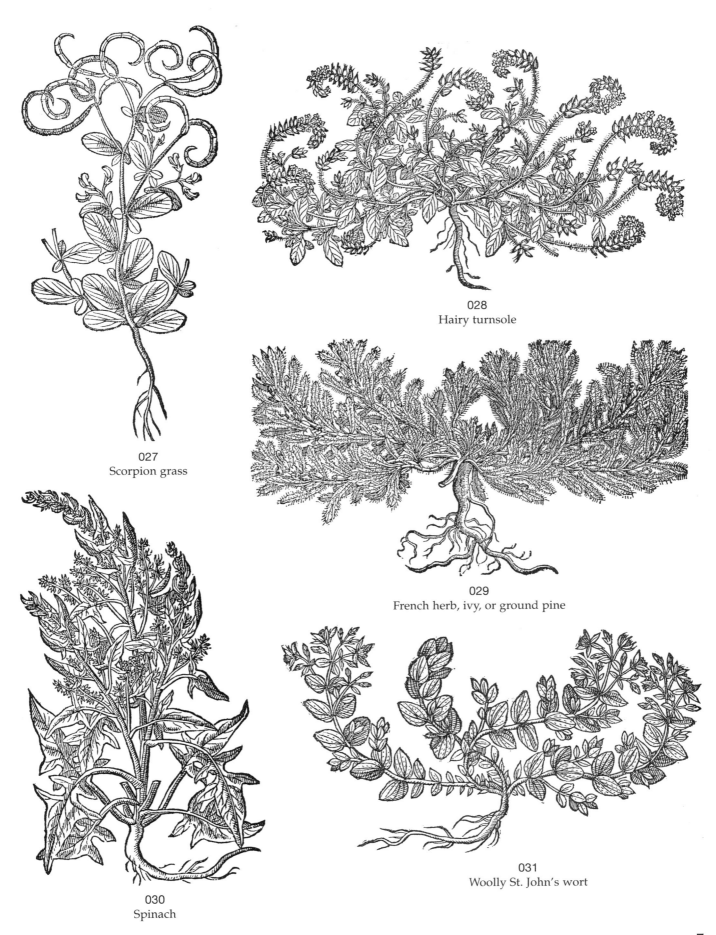

027
Scorpion grass

028
Hairy turnsole

029
French herb, ivy, or ground pine

030
Spinach

031
Woolly St. John's wort

032
Sleepy nightshade

033
Tobacco, or henbane of Peru

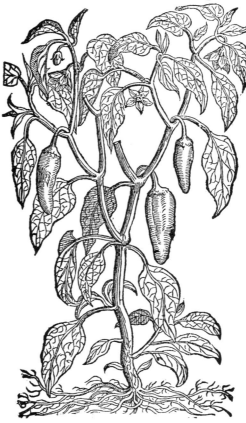

034
Black winter-cherries

035
Long-codded ginnie pepper

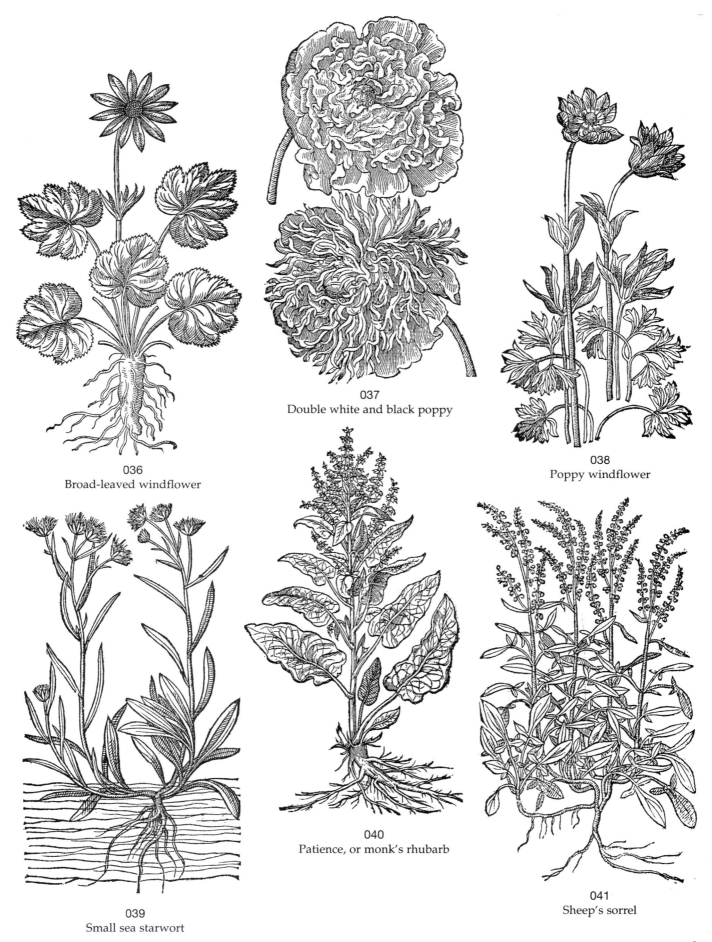

036
Broad-leaved windflower

037
Double white and black poppy

038
Poppy windflower

039
Small sea starwort

040
Patience, or monk's rhubarb

041
Sheep's sorrel

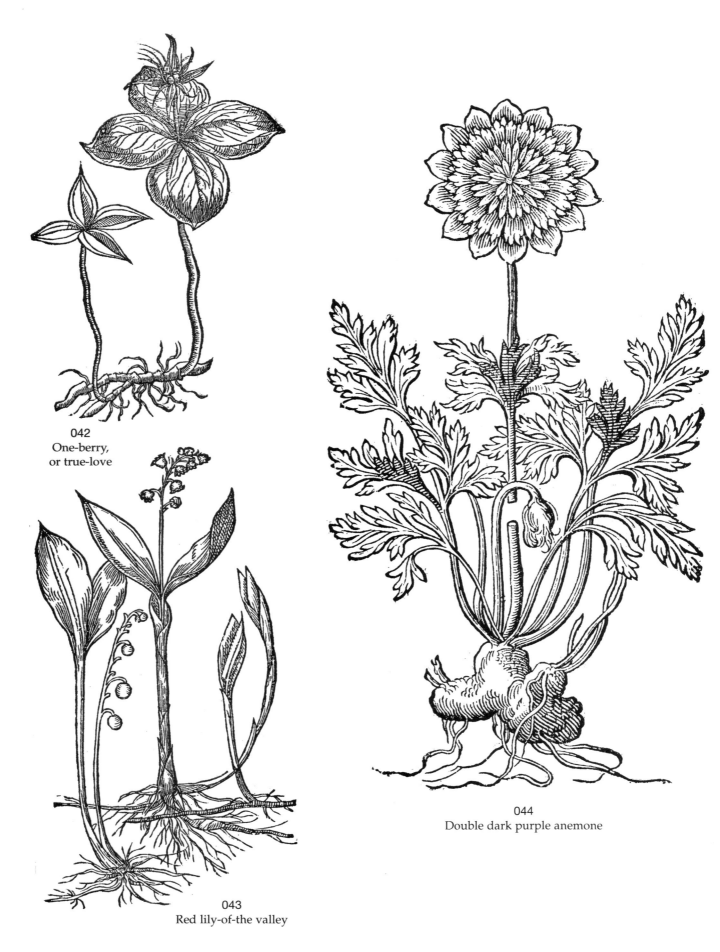

042
One-berry,
or true-love

043
Red lily-of-the valley

044
Double dark purple anemone

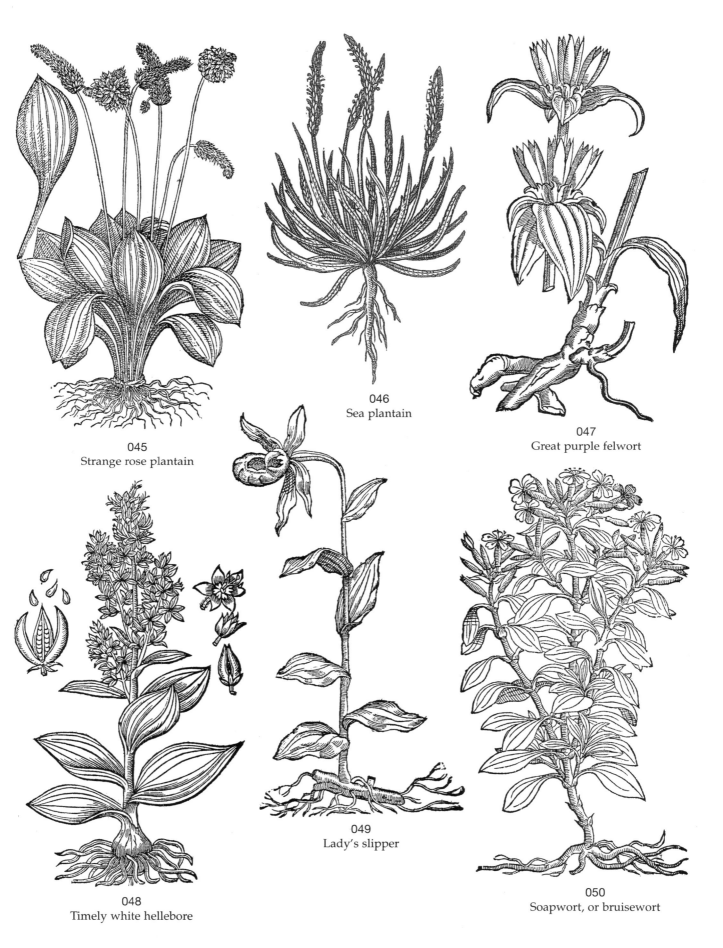

045
Strange rose plantain

046
Sea plantain

047
Great purple felwort

048
Timely white hellebore

049
Lady's slipper

050
Soapwort, or bruisewort

11

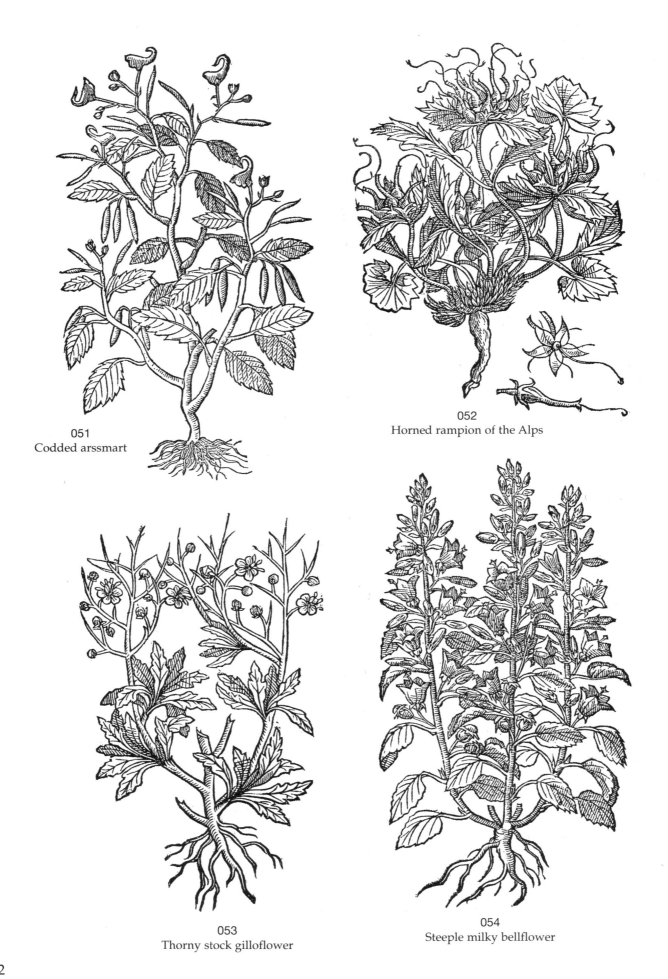

051
Codded arssmart

052
Horned rampion of the Alps

053
Thorny stock gilloflower

054
Steeple milky bellflower

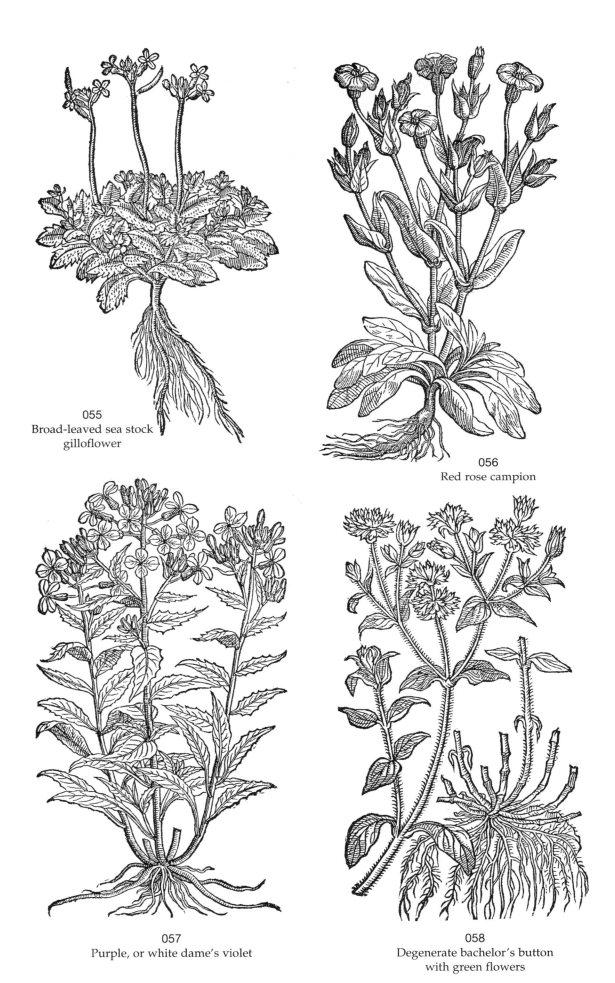

055
Broad-leaved sea stock
gilloflower

056
Red rose campion

057
Purple, or white dame's violet

058
Degenerate bachelor's button
with green flowers

13

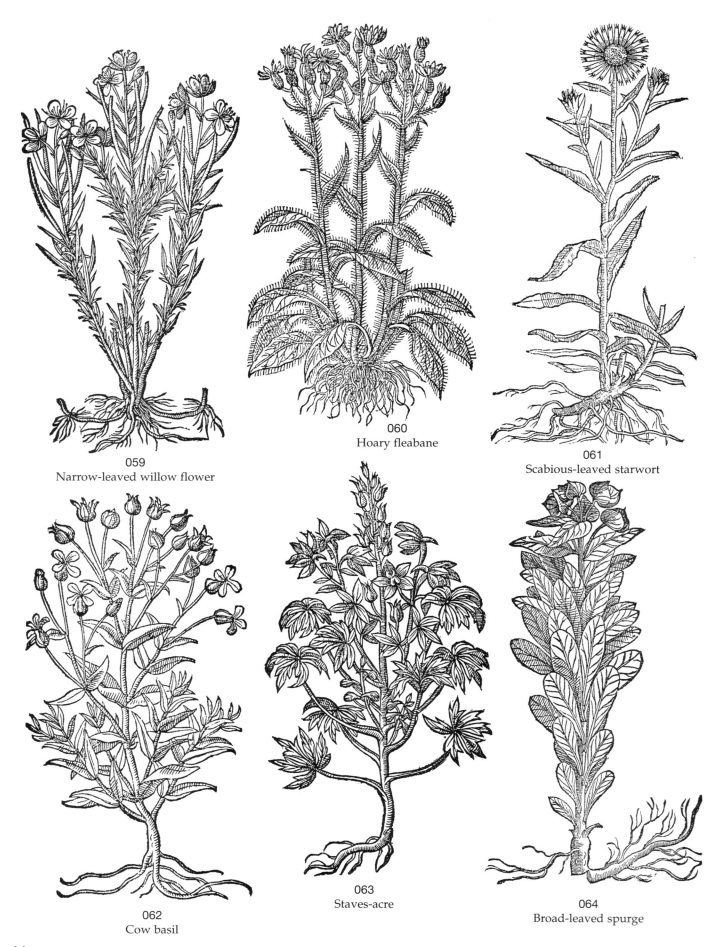

059
Narrow-leaved willow flower

060
Hoary fleabane

061
Scabious-leaved starwort

062
Cow basil

063
Staves-acre

064
Broad-leaved spurge

14

065
Prickly herb aloe, or sea houseleek

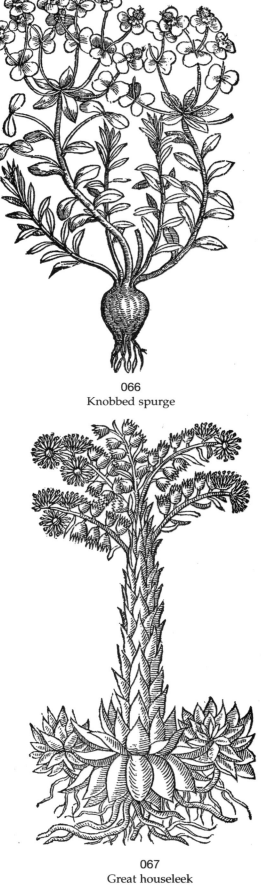

066
Knobbed spurge

067
Great houseleek

068
Small summer sengreen

069
Garden purslane

070
Spanish orpine

071
Italian bastard navelwort

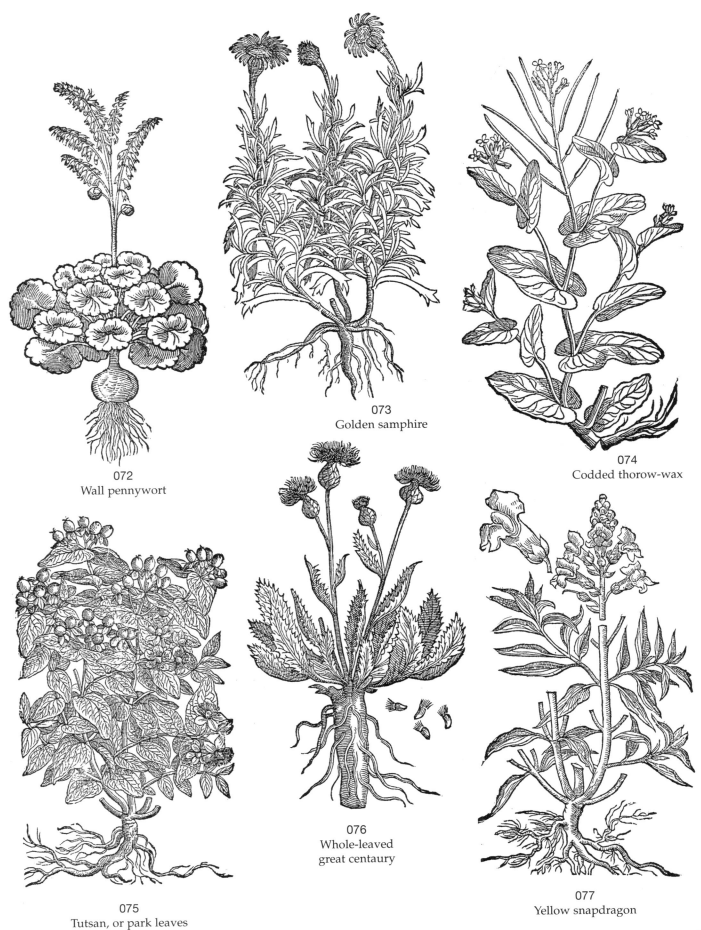

072
Wall pennywort

073
Golden samphire

074
Codded thorow-wax

075
Tutsan, or park leaves

076
Whole-leaved
great centaury

077
Yellow snapdragon

078
Four-leaved creeping toadflax

079
Broad-leaved wild flax

080
Great, or broad-leaved thyme

081
Summer savory

082
Common lavender

083
Sticadove, or stichados

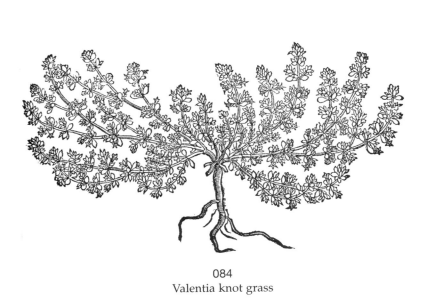

084
Valentia knot grass

086
Great double carnation

085
Purple poly

088
Male crow flower

087
Water crowfoot

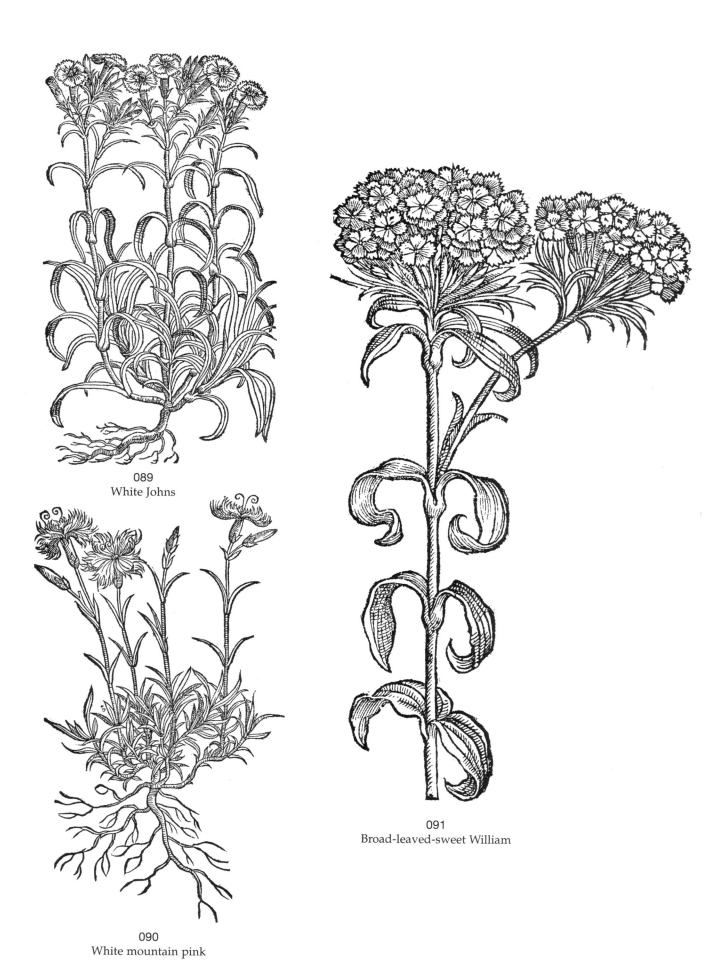

089
White Johns

090
White mountain pink

091
Broad-leaved-sweet William

20

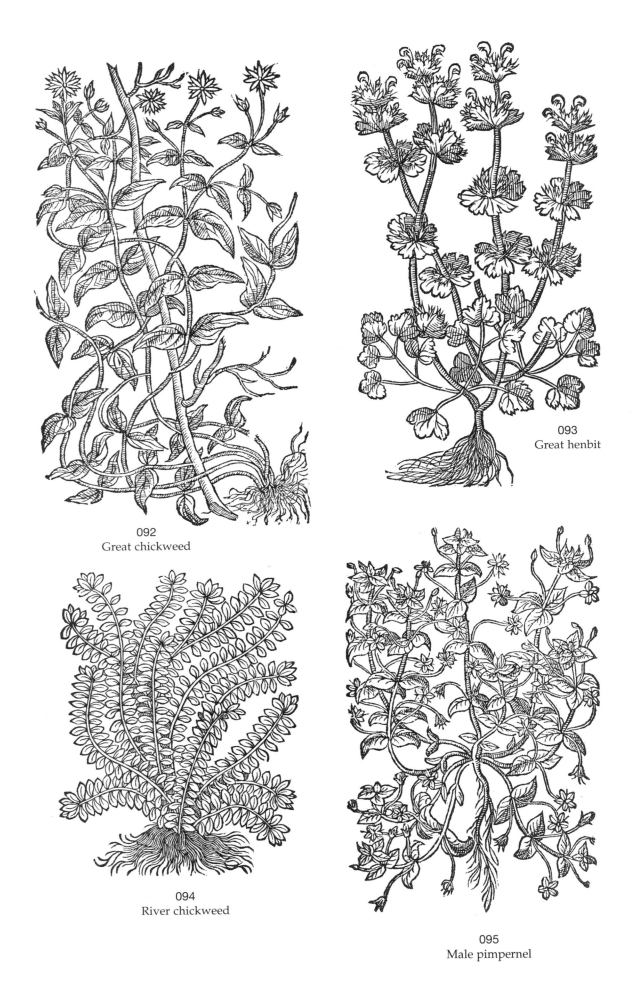

092
Great chickweed

093
Great henbit

094
River chickweed

095
Male pimpernel

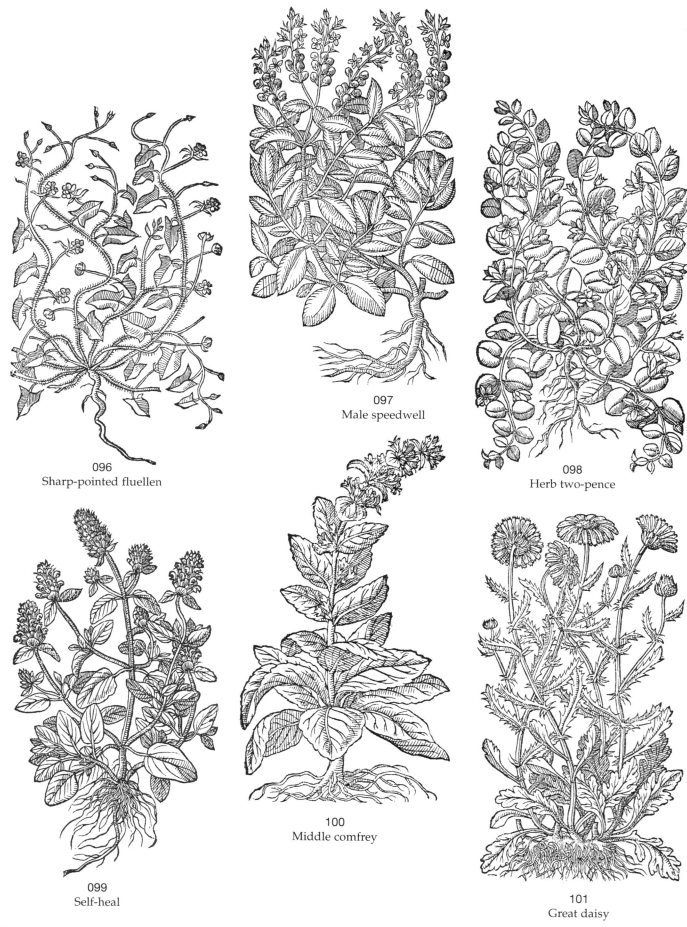

096
Sharp-pointed fluellen

097
Male speedwell

098
Herb two-pence

099
Self-heal

100
Middle comfrey

101
Great daisy

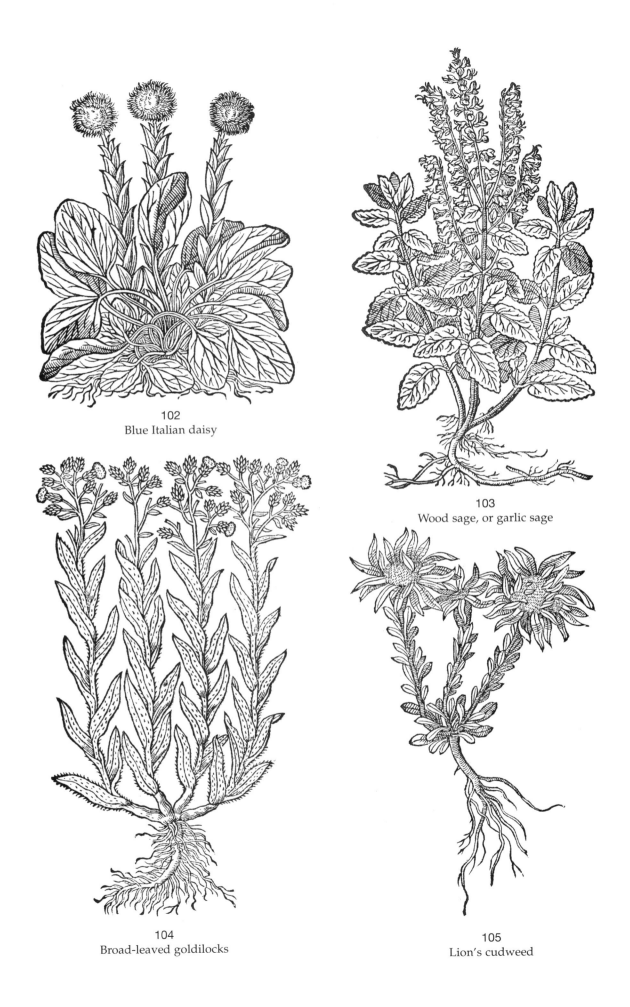

102
Blue Italian daisy

103
Wood sage, or garlic sage

104
Broad-leaved goldilocks

105
Lion's cudweed

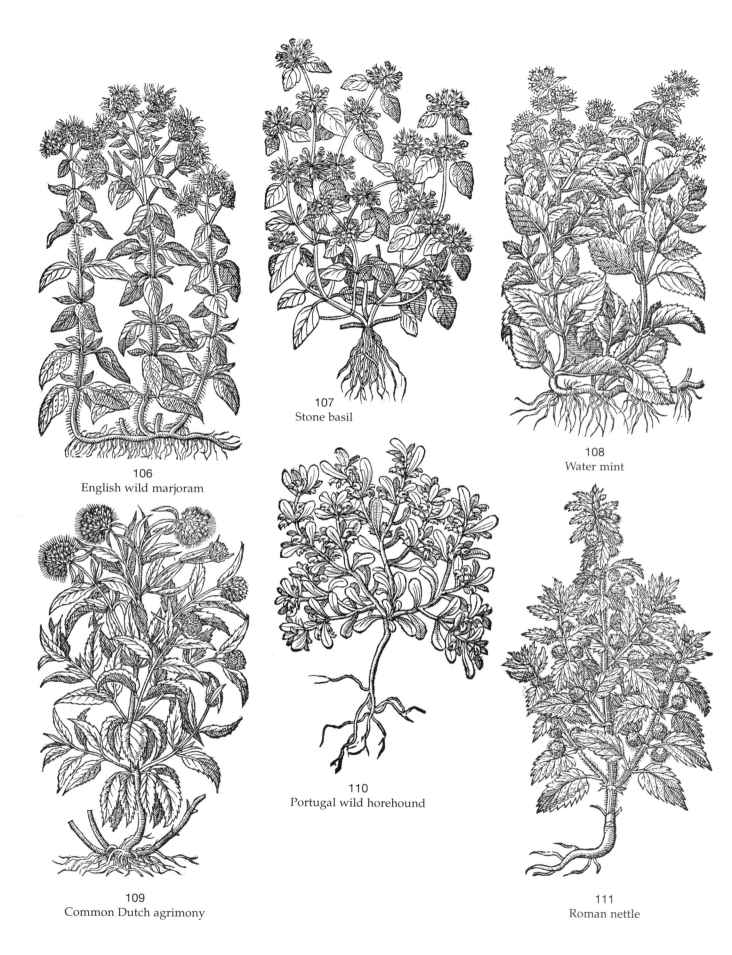

107
Stone basil

108
Water mint

106
English wild marjoram

110
Portugal wild horehound

109
Common Dutch agrimony

111
Roman nettle

112
Bastard balm with purple flowers

113
Betony

114
Bastard hemp

25

115
Yellow-flowered figwort

116
Small creeping blue bottle

117
Devil's bit

118
Knobbed knapweed

119
Strange scabious

120
Yellow goat's-beard

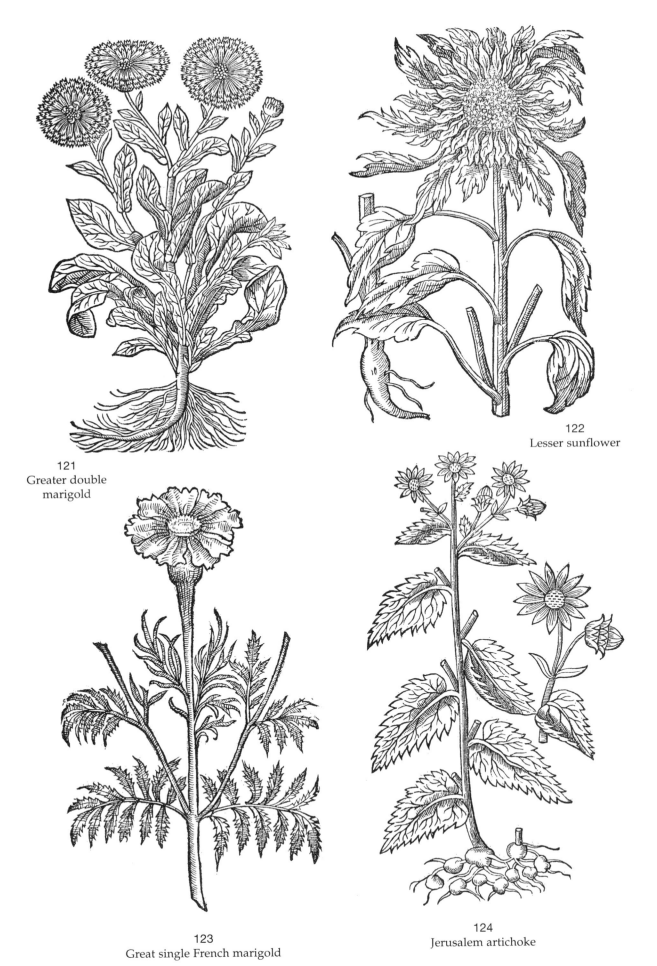

121
Greater double
marigold

122
Lesser sunflower

123
Great single French marigold

124
Jerusalem artichoke

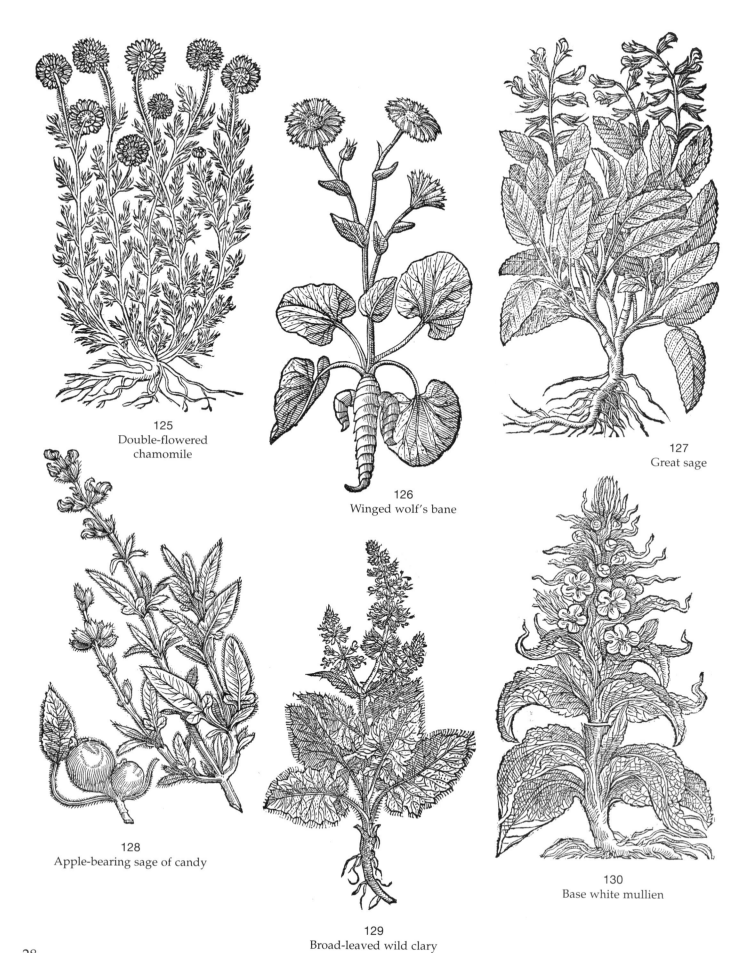

125
Double-flowered
chamomile

126
Winged wolf's bane

127
Great sage

128
Apple-bearing sage of candy

129
Broad-leaved wild clary

130
Base white mullien

131
Moth mullien

132
Mr. Hesketh's primrose

133
Blush-colored bear's ear

29

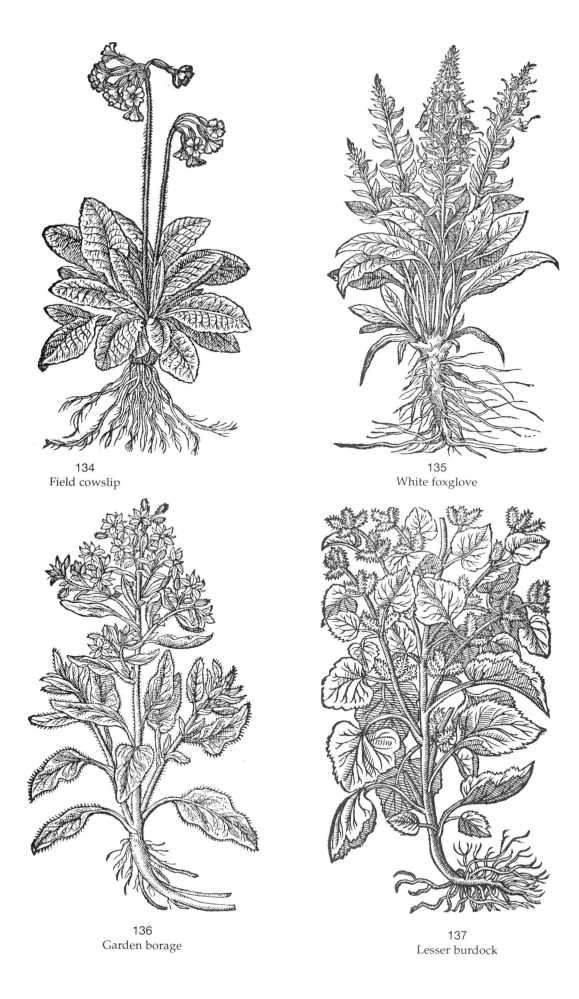

134
Field cowslip

135
White foxglove

136
Garden borage

137
Lesser burdock

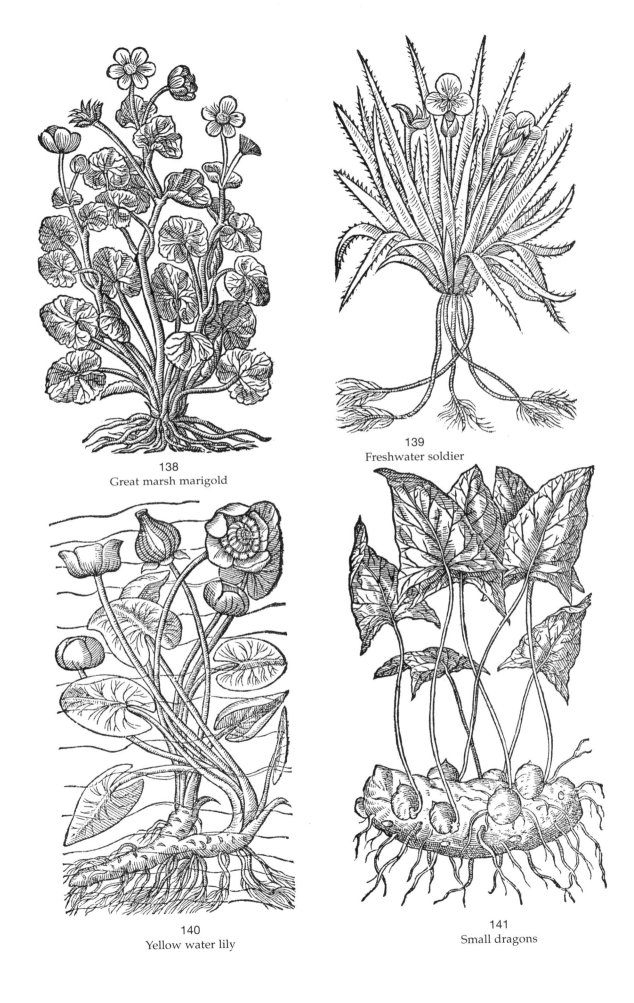

138
Great marsh marigold

139
Freshwater soldier

140
Yellow water lily

141
Small dragons

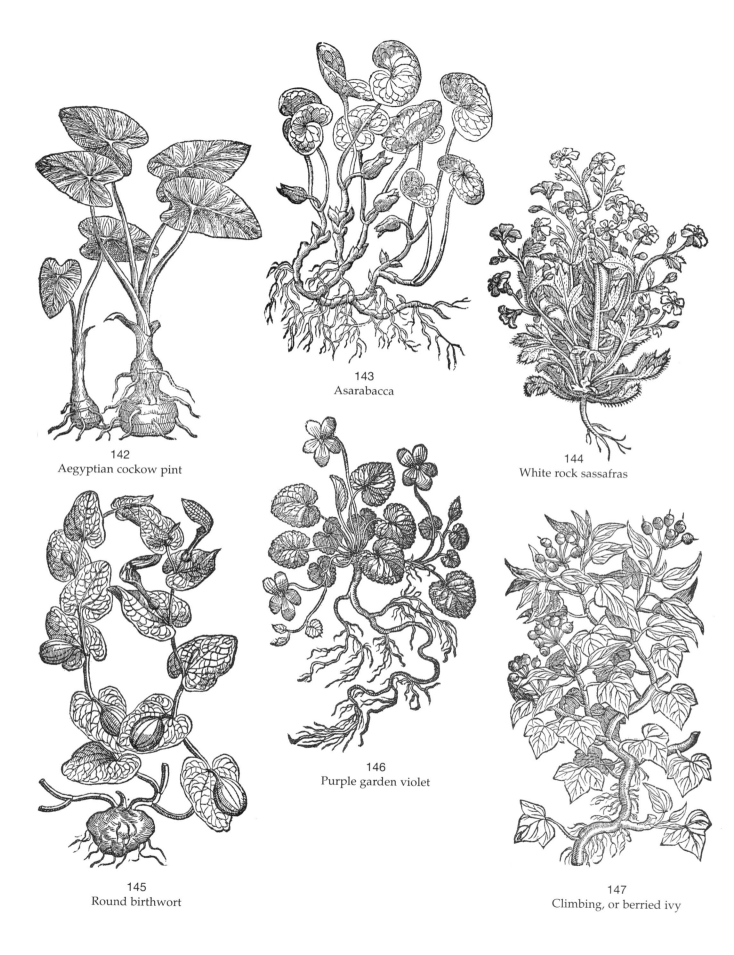

142
Aegyptian cockow pint

143
Asarabacca

144
White rock sassafras

145
Round birthwort

146
Purple garden violet

147
Climbing, or berried ivy

148
Wild pansy

149
Briony of Peru

150
Great buckler pompion

151
Manured vine

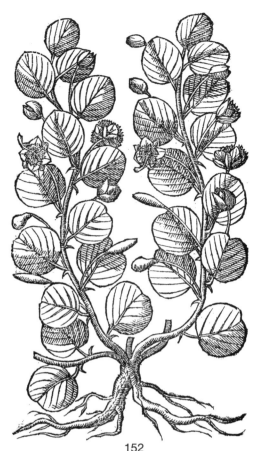

152
Round-leaved capers

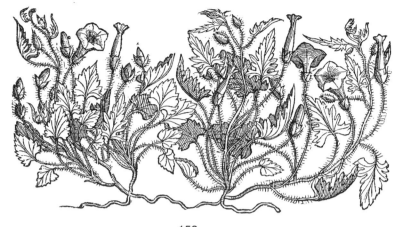

153
Silver-leaved bindweed

154
Square crimson velvet pea

155
Double-flowered virgin's bower

156
Medick fodder of the sea

157
Black swallow-wort

158
Broad-leaved dog's-bane

159
Virginia silk grass

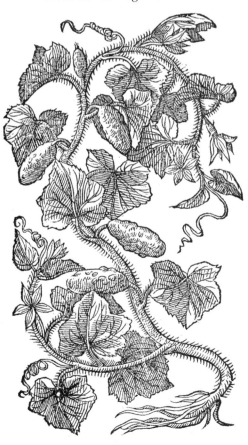

160
Common cucumber

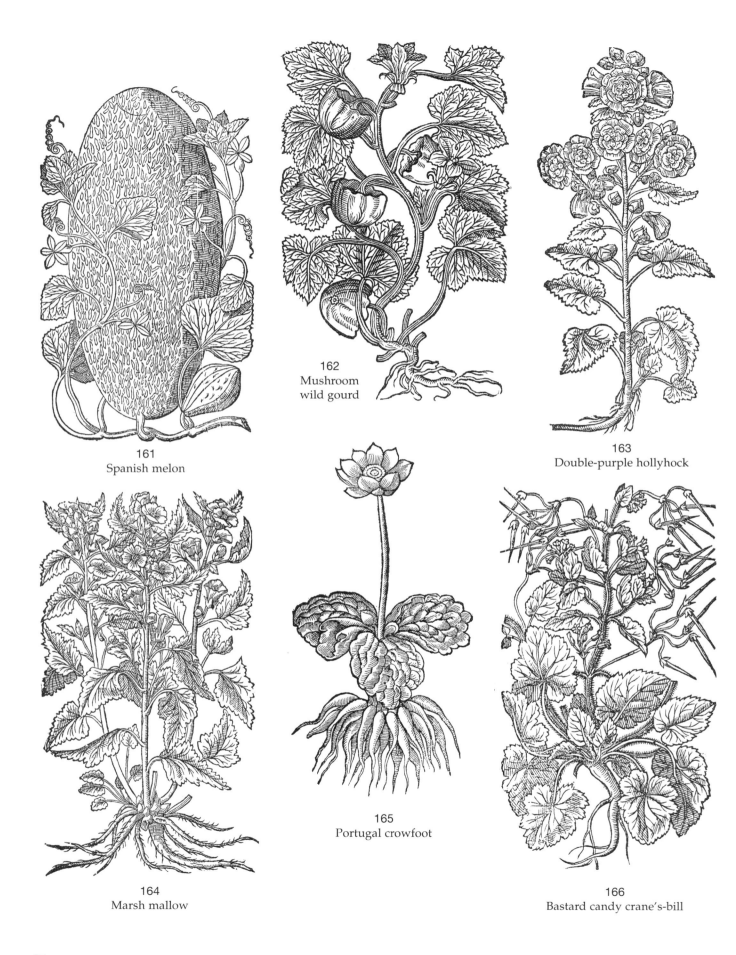

161
Spanish melon

162
Mushroom
wild gourd

163
Double-purple hollyhock

164
Marsh mallow

165
Portugal crowfoot

166
Bastard candy crane's-bill

167
Broad-leaved wolf's bane

168
Double Asian scarlet crowfoot

169
Double red peony

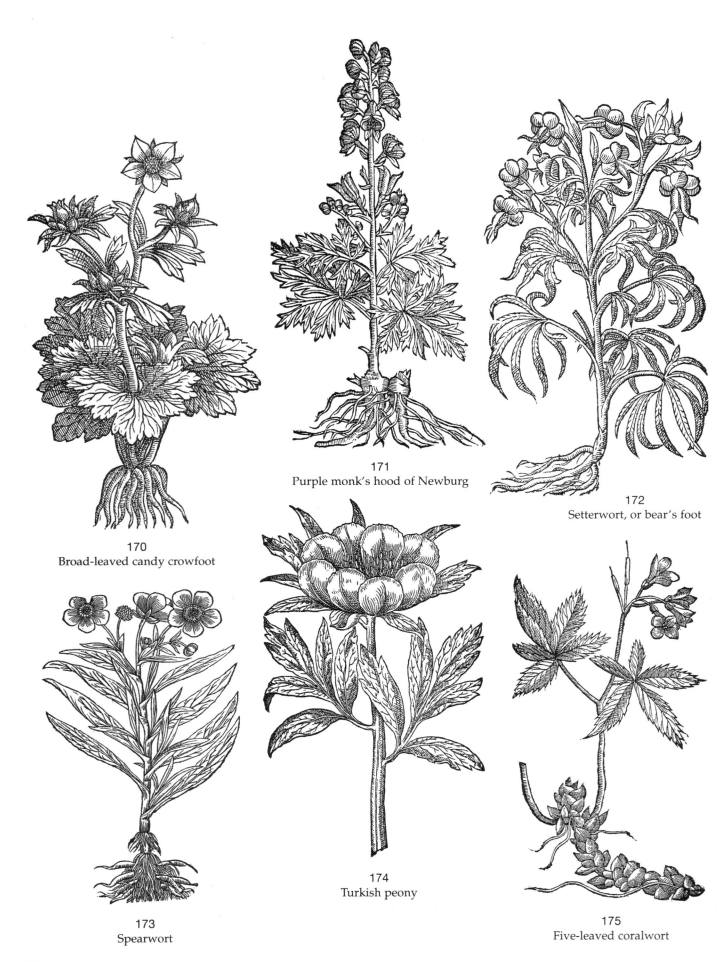

170
Broad-leaved candy crowfoot

171
Purple monk's hood of Newburg

172
Setterwort, or bear's foot

173
Spearwort

174
Turkish peony

175
Five-leaved coralwort

176
Setwall

177
Hercules's great
woundwort

178
Red strawberry

179
Black herb frankincense

180
Garden parsnips

181
Garden parsley

182
Skirrets

183
Wild carrot, or bee's nest

184
Common fennel

185
Dill

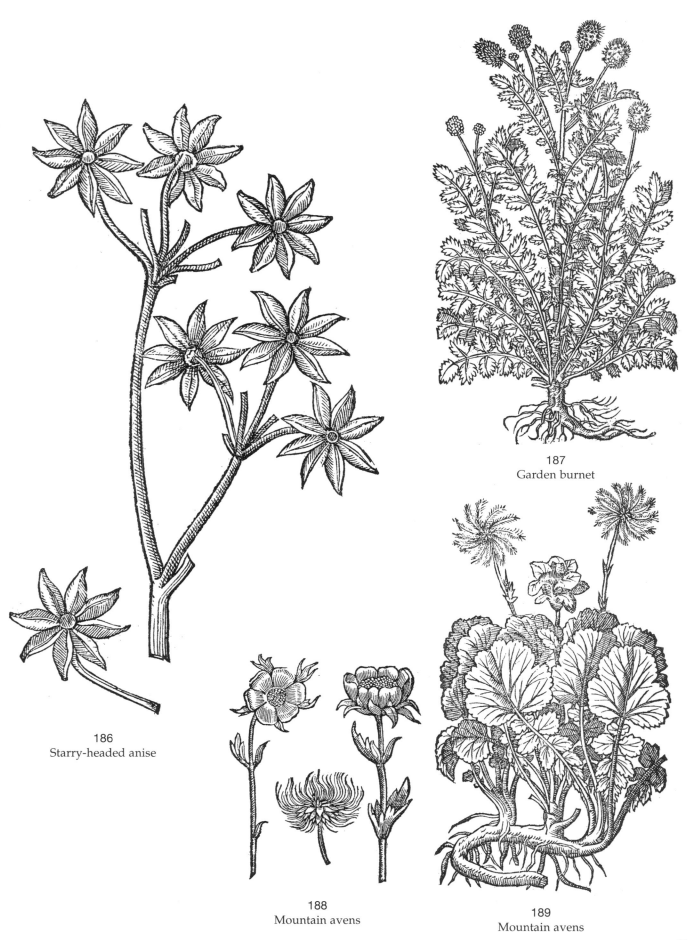

186
Starry-headed anise

187
Garden burnet

188
Mountain avens

189
Mountain avens

41

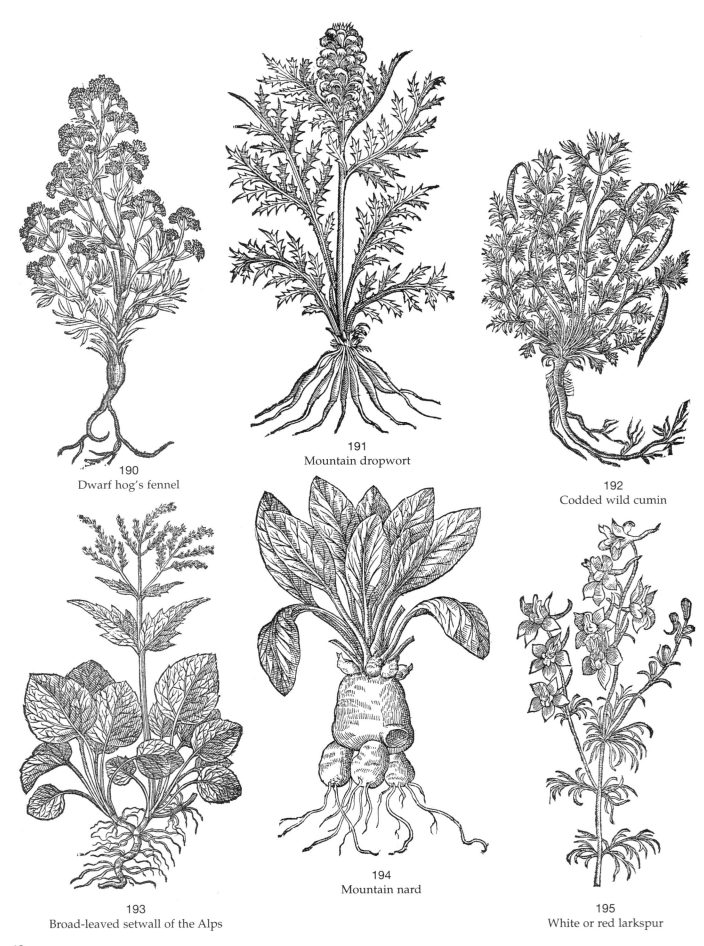

190
Dwarf hog's fennel

191
Mountain dropwort

192
Codded wild cumin

193
Broad-leaved setwall of the Alps

194
Mountain nard

195
White or red larkspur

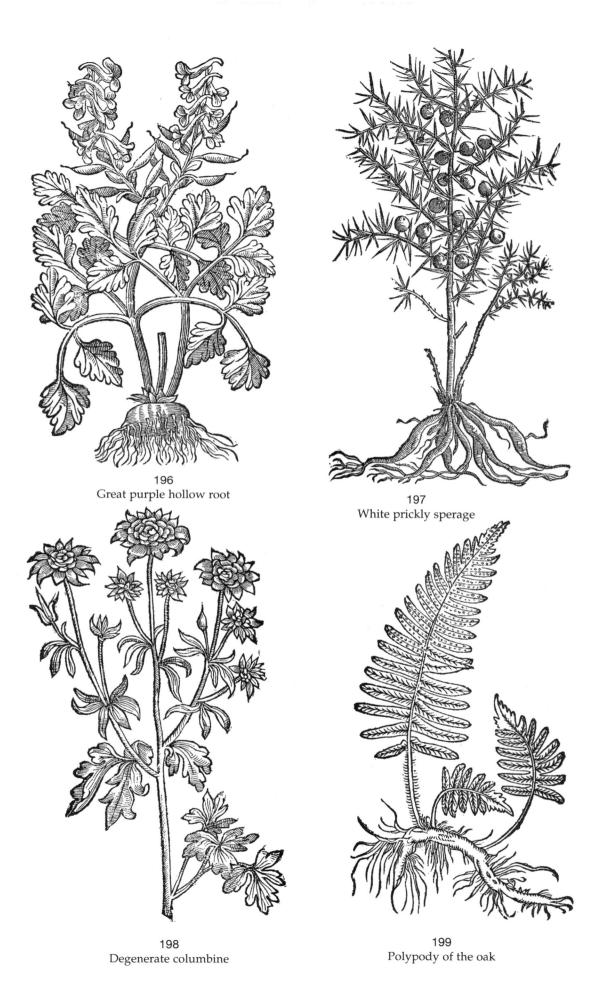

196
Great purple hollow root

197
White prickly sperage

198
Degenerate columbine

199
Polypody of the oak

43

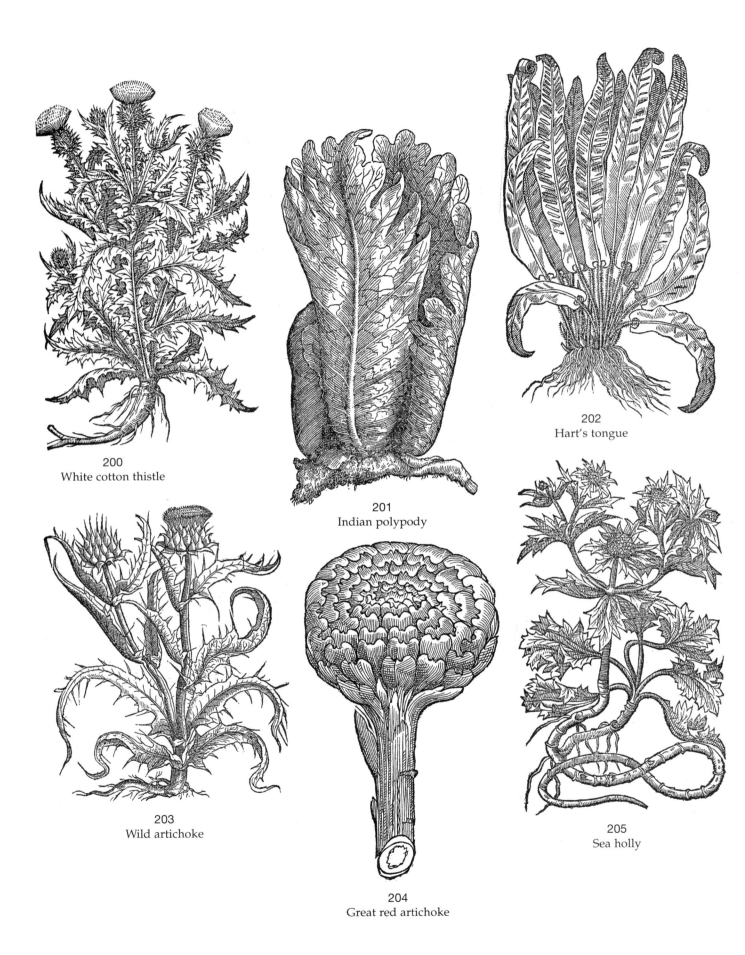

200
White cotton thistle

201
Indian polypody

202
Hart's tongue

203
Wild artichoke

204
Great red artichoke

205
Sea holly

44

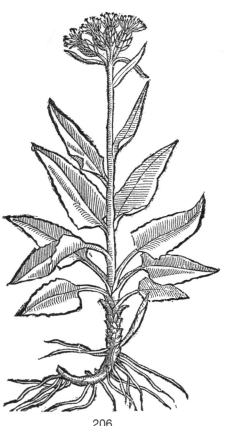

206
Dock-leaved thistle-gentle

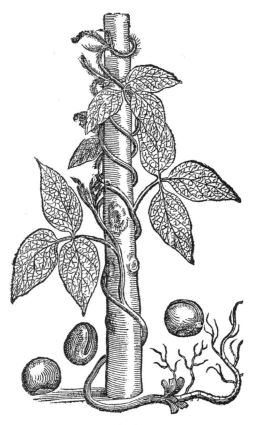

207
Kidney bean of Brazil

208
Meadow trefoil

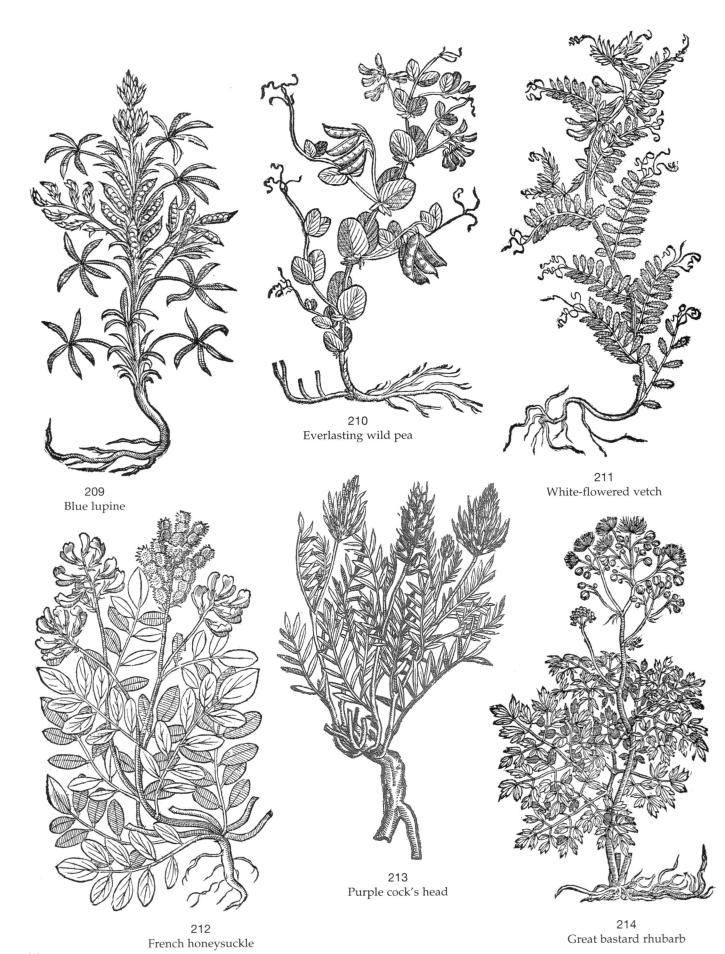

210
Everlasting wild pea

211
White-flowered vetch

209
Blue lupine

213
Purple cock's head

212
French honeysuckle

214
Great bastard rhubarb

INDEX